SHE WILL STAND AS A *BEACON,* SHINING EVEN BRIGHTER THAN THE STAR THAT IS *MY METROPOLIS,* LIGHTING THE WAY FOR *MANKIND* EVERYWHERE.

SOLUTIONS ARE NOT EASY TO COME BY. THEY DON'T PRESENT THEMSELVES, NEATLY WRAPPED IN COLORFUL PAPER.

LIKE ANY THING OF VALUE, THEY HAVE TO BE DUG FOR, SOMETIMES IN THE HARDEST GROUND TO BREAK...

...ONE'S OWN HUMAN CLAY.

MORE OFTEN THAN NOT, MINING ONE'S SELF LEADS TO FOOL'S GOLD, UNLESS THE PICK IS TAKEN TO ONE'S PRIDE. ONE MUST BREAK OFF A CHUNK, AND SWALLOW IT...

...A BITTER PILL, FOR A BETTER TOMORROW.

I'LL BE GETTING IN LATE, YOU DON'T HAVE TO MEET ME.

YOU DON'T HAVE TO. BUT DINNER SOUNDS NICE. AND IT'S JUST DINNER, RIGHT?

I MEAN YOU HAVE A REPUTATION.

NO SURPRISES OKAY?

"...NOT *INHERITED.*"

MORE OFTEN THAN NOT, WHEN CHOOSING A PATH, IT'S THE *EASY* ROAD THAT'S TAKEN.

THE REASONS ARE *OBVIOUS.* UNDERSTANDABLE...

...BUT ULTIMATELY, *UNDEFENDABLE.*

BECAUSE WE WERE *CREATED* TO CREATE *OURSELVES...*

IT'S THE *GREATEST GIFT OUR* CREATOR GAVE TO US.

THE PROBLEM THOUGH, IS THAT FOR MANY, A GIFT *FALLS SHORT* OF WHAT THEY BELIEVE THEY *DESERVE.*

...AND *DESIRE* MEANS THERE'S A *HOLE* IN THE MAN.

I WONDER, NOT JUST *WHAT* THAT HOLE IS...

...BUT *HOW DEEP* IT IS.

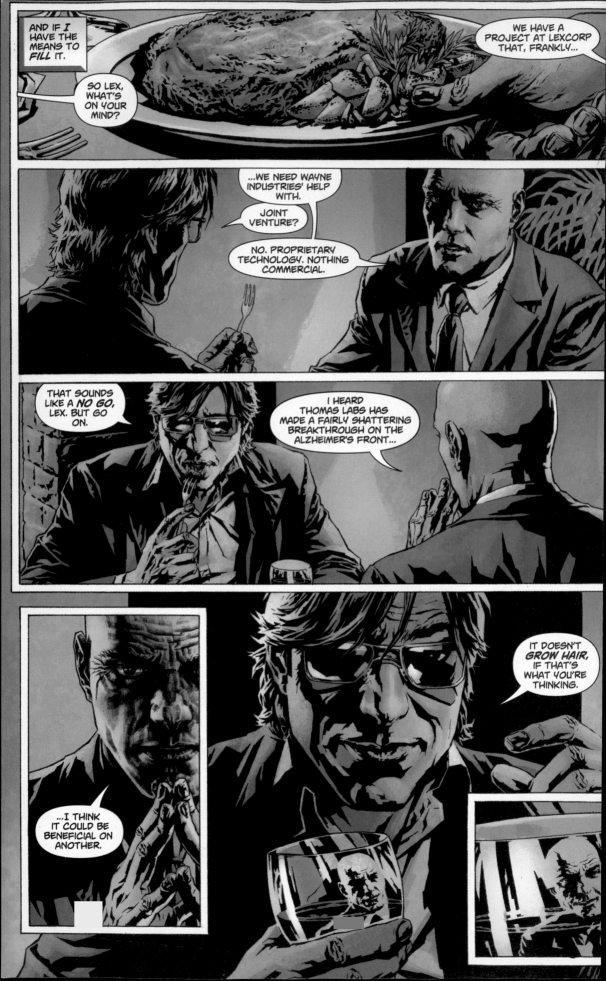

"...CAN YOU SAY THE SAME?"

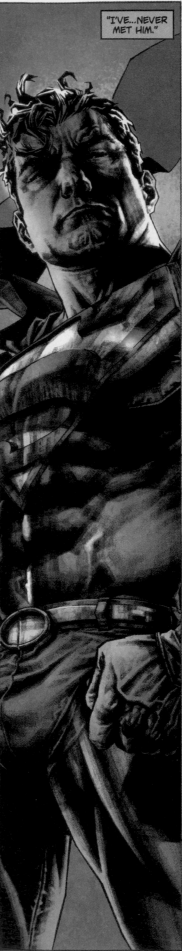

"I'VE...NEVER MET HIM."

"YOU DON'T MEET *IT*--IT MEETS *YOU*. HEAD ON, AND I' BUCKLES YOUR KNEES, LIKE / FORCE OF NATURE--

"--BUT IT ISN'T *NATURAL*."

"IT" HAS A
[NA]ME, LEX--"

"--THAT *WE* GAVE HIM, AN ATTEMPT TO HUMANIZE HIM--AS POINTLESS AS NAMING A HURRICANE.

"FORGET THE NAME, BRUCE..."

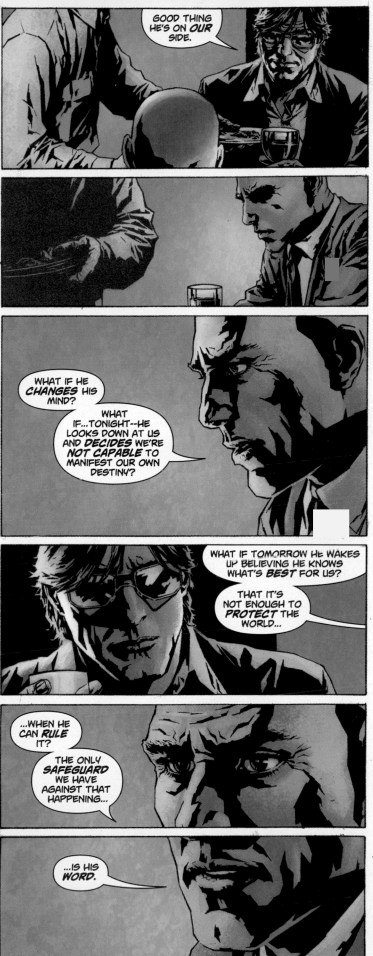

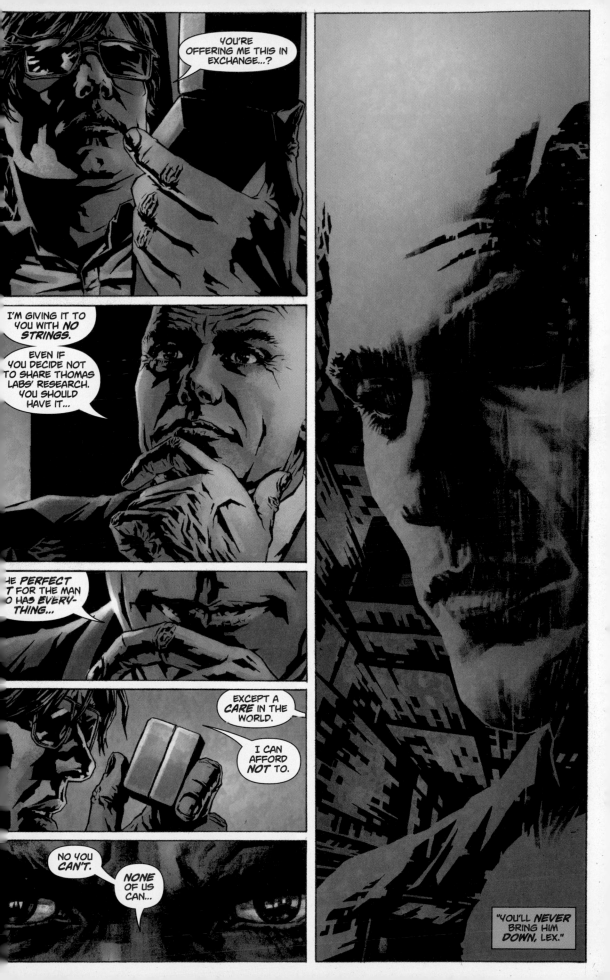

SO THE MYTHIC MUST BE *EXPOSED* FOR WHAT IT *IS.*

SO WE CAN BELIEVE IN *OURSELVES.*

BECAUSE IT'S ONLY WHAT'S *IN* US...

...THE *DRIVE* TO BE MYTHIC...

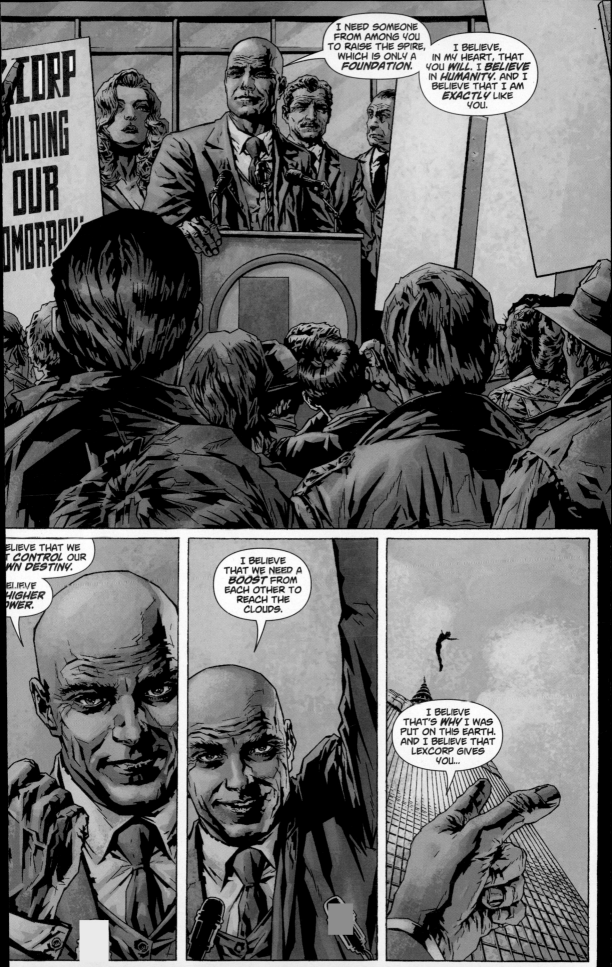

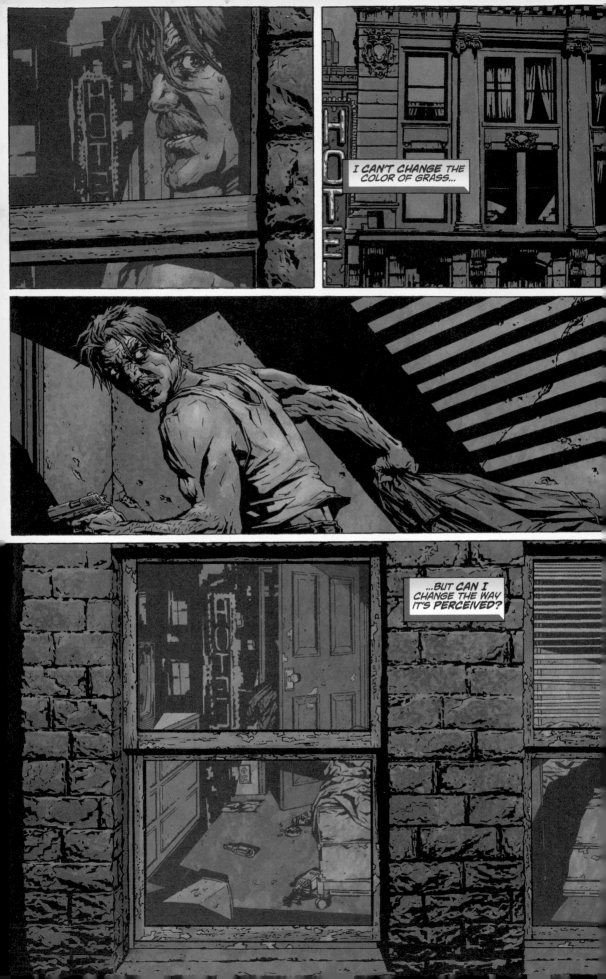

...FEAR.

RIGHT NOW, EVERY CITIZEN IN METROPOLIS IS GLUED TO THEIR TELEVISION, WANTING DESPERATELY FOR SOMEONE OF STRENGTH TO MAKE THAT FEAR GO AWAY.

AND LIKE AN AVENGING ANGEL SHE SWOOPS DOWN...

WINSLOW--ON HIS BEST DAY--WAS NOTHING BUT A PETTY CRIMINAL AND A FAILED HUMAN BEING.

I MADE HIM A MONSTER.

THIS CITY FEARS HIM, AND IT WATCHES, HOPING FOR ONE THING...

D'S TVA

CLICK

JUSTICE.

BUT THEN, HOPE IS AN ASPIRATION.

A BEACON THAT SHINES BRIGHTER THAN ANY STAR, LIGHTING THE WAY FOR ALL MANKIND.

0Q111DHH_JUFJJNWMNDM093762
0001000100110110000100...JWY
00Q1111KSDHH1KSDHH_JUFJJNWM
762 000100010011011000010000

AUTO-DESTRUCT_

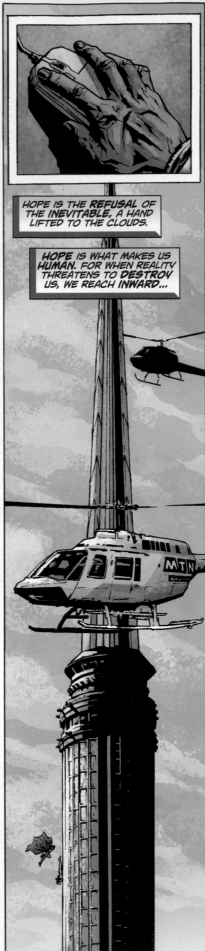

HOPE IS THE REFUSAL OF THE INEVITABLE, A HAND LIFTED TO THE CLOUDS.

HOPE IS WHAT MAKES US HUMAN. FOR WHEN REALITY THREATENS TO DESTROY US, WE REACH INWARD...

...AND WE CREATE HOPE.

IT'S THE GREATEST GIFT WE CAN GIVE EACH OTHER.

THOUGH, IT JUST MAY BE THE FOUNDATION....

0Q111DHH_JUFJJNWMNDM093762
0001...101100001000...JW
000...KSDHH1KSDHH_JUFJJNW
762...01011000100

DETONATE